THE B!G QUEST

PRESENTS

WHAT MAKES BEING ORIGINAL SO ICONIC?

A DAILY PAPER STORY

FEATURING

JEFFERSON OSEI

CO-FOUNDER OF DAILY PAPER

The Big Question™

What makes being original so iconic?

Published by Adventurous Publishing
Copyright © 2024 Jefferson Osei

Paperback ISBN: 978-1-915862-45-7
Hardback ISBN: 978-1-915862-44-0

Welcome to this edition on

Originality

Ft # Jefferson Osei

Co - Founder - Daily Paper

Contents

THE B!G QUESTION.

Our why

The Big Question is a brand that delve's deep into the minds of influential leaders and uncover their strategies through asking Big questions.

We believe that the journey from aspiration to achievement is both fascinating and instructive.

By asking leaders profound questions about their experiences, we gain valuable insights that can guide you in turning your own dreams into tangible outcomes.

Welcome to this edition in The Big Question book series on Originality.

In this book we speak to Jefferson Osei, a co-founder of the rising phenomenon fashion brand Daily Paper, based in Amsterdam.

In this book we'll look at the Daily Paper story, and why true originality goes unmatched.

Introduction

Beginnings

Where does it begin—the pursuit of what we call originality? Origins, after all, are rarely as pure as we like to imagine. They hide in the shadows of something older, something long forgotten, a twisted reflection of what came before. Every great idea, every so-called invention, has roots deep beneath the surface, tangled in a web of stolen moments and borrowed thoughts.

We like to believe that originality springs forth from nothing, that it's a spark igniting in the darkness of the mind. But what if it's simply the clever rearrangement of pieces that were always there?

What if every origin is merely a repurposing of what was, a trick of the mind convincing us that what's new was never seen before?

And yet, we are drawn to it, compelled to seek out these beginnings, as if uncovering them will somehow make sense of the chaos. Originality is often perceived as a mysterious force, a quality that sets certain ideas, creations, or people apart from the rest.

It's something admired, sought after, and revered, yet its true nature can be elusive.

I'm Jefferson osei, and this is a Daily Paper, origins story.

Chapter *one*

Origins

Originality, at its core, is about beginnings.

The word itself finds its roots in the Latin originem, meaning "beginning, source, birth." This origin story is not just a linguistic curiosity but a key to understanding the essence of originality.

It suggests that to be original is to be a source, a starting point from which something new and unique emerges.

Daily Paper's story began in a similar way – as a source, a beginning that was deeply connected to our roots. It started as a simple blog, a digital canvas where my friends and I could showcase the vibrant creative scene in Amsterdam. We were just three friends of Ghanaian, Somali, and Moroccan descent, united by our love for storytelling and our desire to fill a void in the representation of our city's culture. Initially, fashion wasn't even on our radar.

Creating daily paper was more about expressing our personal tastes and styles thus celebrating the diverse influences that shaped us.

But language, like creativity, evolves. Over time, the concept of originality has expanded, taking on new shades of meaning. It is no longer just about being the first; it is about being the first in a way that matters.

It's about creating something that not only didn't exist before but also couldn't have existed without the unique perspective and voice of the creator. In our case, this evolution led us to fashion, where we could channel our creativity into something tangible, something that told our stories in a way that words alone couldn't.

From the earliest storytellers to modern innovators, the quest for originality has driven us to explore, to experiment, and to push the boundaries of what is possible. Yet, this quest is not without its challenges.

To be truly original often means to go against the grain, to take risks, and to face the unknown. This was true for us at Daily Paper, as we transitioned from a blog to a fashion brand, blending African heritage with contemporary streetwear.

THE B!G QUESTION.

Chapter *two*

Finding Purpose

So, what does it really mean to be original?

At a glance, originality might seem synonymous with novelty – the creation of something new. But if we look closer, we find that originality is about more than just newness. It's about bringing forth something that is not only new but also significant, something that carries with it a sense of purpose and authenticity.

Novelty is the first step on the path to originality. It's the initial spark that catches our attention, the sense of discovering something we've never encountered before. In a world where so much has already been done, novelty can be thrilling. It invites curiosity, challenges our assumptions, and opens our minds to new possibilities.

This was the case when we first began experimenting with fashion. It was a new direction for us, an uncharted territory where we could express our creativity in ways we hadn't before.

But novelty alone does not make something original. Just because something is new doesn't mean it has depth or resonance.

For originality to truly captivate, it must go beyond the surface, touching on something more profound.

Chapter *three*

Authenticity

Authenticity is where the true power of originality lies. It's the pulse that gives originality life, the core that grounds it in something real and meaningful. Authenticity is about being true to oneself, expressing ideas that are genuine and unfiltered by external expectations. For me, growing up in a household where I was encouraged to stay connected to my Ghanaian roots, authenticity became the wellspring of my creativity.

It influenced everything from the way I dressed to the music I listened to, and it became a guiding principle as we developed Daily Paper.

When originality is rooted in authenticity, it resonates with others on a deeper level. It's not just about creating something different; it's about creating something that feels right, that carries with it the weight of personal truth.

This kind of originality doesn't just stand out; it connects, it moves, it inspires.

Originality doesn't exist in a vacuum.

When a truly original idea takes root, it doesn't just change the creator; it has the power to change the world around it.

This is where originality reveals its full potential – in the impact it has on others.

The early days of Daily Paper were a whirlwind of experimentation and discovery.

Each piece we created was a canvas, telling a story that resonated with people from all walks of life.

The response was overwhelming, and we knew we were onto something special.

THE B!G QUESTION.

Chapter *four*

Storytelling

Storytelling is the lifeblood of originality. In a world where fashion trends come and go with the blink of an eye, it's the stories we weave into our work that breathe life into it, giving it depth and resonance.

When we founded Daily Paper, our mission extended beyond creating a clothing brand; it was about narrating our story. Fashion was merely the medium; our true aim was to encapsulate our heritage, identity, and vision for the future.

As people of African descent, our roots are intricately interlaced with everything we produce. The richness of our culture, the depth of our history, and the vibrancy of our heritage infuse every piece of clothing we create. Growing up in a world where African narratives were often marginalised or distorted, we felt a profound need to reclaim and redefine that story.

Storytelling through fashion became not just a creative choice but an imperative. Our heritage is our cornerstone, and true originality springs from an unyielding commitment to where we come from, while reimagining it for the contemporary world.

Daily Paper was conceived as more than just a fashion label; it was a cultural movement. We sought to reveal the depth of Afrocentric culture—not through a lens of tradition or nostalgia, but through a modern, edgy perspective.

Every collection we launch is more than apparel; it is a narrative of our ancestors, our communities, and our aspirations. It's about presenting our heritage as a living, breathing entity that continues to evolve and influence the culture around us.

The connection people feel with us transcends beyond the bold prints, intricate patterns, or standout designs. It's the narrative behind these elements that resonates deeply.

Wearing Daily Paper is more than donning a jacket or hoodie; it's embodying a story, a piece of history reinterpreted for the streets of today.

Throughout the years, we've partnered with musicians (W*iz kid, Beyonce, Burna boy and more*), athletes, and creatives who share our vision. Figures like Kendrick Lamar, whose fusion of art and activism mirrors our ethos, or Virgil van Dijk, who exemplifies excellence both on and off the field.

Our collaborations are never superficial; they merge our stories with theirs, creating something that echoes on a profound level.

We've also aligned with other brands that grasp the essence of storytelling. Whether through limited-edition capsules or expansive collaborations, we always strive to advance the narrative.

We're not interested in mimicking trends or duplicating existing formulas. Our goal is to forge something unique and unparalleled.

Our storytelling extends beyond the clothing itself. We craft narratives through visuals—our photoshoots, social media presence, and public personas all reflect the cultures and histories that inspire us.

Daily Paper is more than fashion; it's a way of life. Each campaign, each video, and each image is meticulously designed to voice untold stories and share them with the world.

For us, authenticity is the wellspring of originality. It's not something we chase or fabricate; it's inherent in who we are. It's embedded in our upbringing, our experiences, and the stories handed down through generations.

That's the essence of Daily Paper—we're not about chasing fleeting trends; we're about remaining true to ourselves and the stories we carry. True originality emerges from the courage to tell your own story, in your own voice, and with unwavering pride.

THE B!G QUESTION.

My big question to you is...

Whats **holding you back?**

About the author

Jefferson Osei is a co-founder and the creative director of Daily Paper, a renowned fashion brand that celebrates Afrocentric culture through modern streetwear. His work is celebrated for its fusion of traditional African heritage with contemporary fashion trends, aiming to tell the rich stories of African communities and history.

Born and raised in Amsterdam, Osei and his partners established Daily Paper with the goal of creating a fashion label that reflects their heritage and personal stories. His role as creative director involves shaping the brand's identity through design, collaborations, and storytelling, ensuring that each collection is deeply rooted in cultural narratives while appealing to a global audience.

Daily Paper Co-founders, **Jefferson Osei**, *top left*, **Abdeljelil "Jill" Azzouzi**, *bottom left, and* **Hafid Koudou**, *right.*

THE B!G QUESTION.

Be **you**,
be **bold**,
Go **big**.

TBQ

Notes

...............Go big

..............Go big

..............Go big

...............Go big

_____

_____

_____

_____

_____

_____

_____

_____

_____

_____

_____

_____

_____

_____

_____

_____

_____

_____.............Go big

...............Go big

...............Go big

..............Go big

_____
_____
_____
_____
_____
_____
_____
_____
_____
_____
_____
_____
_____
_____
_____
_____
_____
_____
_____..............Go big

_____

_____

_____

_____

_____

_____

_____

_____

_____

_____

_____

_____

_____

_____

_____

_____

_____

_____..............Go big

...............Go big

..............Go big

................Go big

_____
_____
_____
_____
_____
_____
_____
_____
_____
_____
_____
_____
_____
_____
_____
_____
_____
_____
_____..............Go big

...............Go big

_____

_____

_____

_____

_____

_____

_____

_____

_____

_____

_____

_____

_____

_____

_____..............Go big

_____

_____

_____

_____

_____

_____

_____

_____

_____

_____

_____

_____

_____

_____

_____

_____

_____

_____..............Go big

_____
_____
_____
_____
_____

_____
_____
_____
_____

_____
_____
_____

_____
_____
_____

_____
..............Go big

..............Go big

_____
_____
_____
_____
_____
_____
_____
_____
_____
_____
_____
_____
_____
_____
_____
_____
_____..............Go big

...............Go big

_____

_____

_____

_____

_____

_____

_____

_____

_____

_____

_____

_____

_____

_____..............Go big

..............Go big

..............Go big

...............Go big

_____

_____

_____

_____

_____

_____

_____

_____

_____

_____

_____

_____

_____

_____

_____

_____

_____

_____..............Go big

..............Go big

...............Go big

in The Big Question

O @thebigquestionhq

www.ingramcontent.com/pod-product-compliance
Lightning Source LLC
Chambersburg PA
CBHW071235200326
41521CB00009B/1490